How well do you know Islām?

By
Shaykh Mufti Saiful Islām

JKN Publications

© Copyright by JKN Publications

First Edition May 2011 — 5000 copies
Second Edition September 2016 - 3000 copies

ISBN 978-0-9565504-4-6

British Library Cataloguing in Publication Data
A catalogue record for this book is available from the British Library.

Publisher's Note:

Every care and attention has been put into the production of this book. If however, you find any errors, they are our own, for which we seek Allāh's 🌼 forgiveness and reader's pardon.

Published by:

JKN Publications
118 Manningham Lane
Bradford
West Yorkshire
BD8 7JF
United Kingdom

t: +44 (0) 1274 308 456 | w: www.jkn.org.uk | e: info@jkn.org.uk

Author: Shaykh Mufti Saiful Islām

Printed by Mega Printing in Turkey

"In the Name of Allāh, the Most Beneficent,
the Most Merciful"

Contents

Introduction

بِسْمِ اللهِ الرَّحْمٰنِ الرَّحِيمِ

All praises are for Allāh ﷻ, the Lord of the worlds. And may peace and blessings be upon the beloved Messenger of Allah ﷺ, upon his noble family ؆, his Sahābah ؆, and upon those who follow the True Path until the Day of Judgement.

Having previously authored two educational books; "Hadeeth for Beginners" and "Du'ā for Beginners", Shaykh Mufti Saiful Islām has endeavoured to add to the series another exciting book titled "How well do you know Islām?" This book contains 300 multiple questions and answers to help you increase your knowledge on Islām!

Identifying a greater need to publish educational material in the English language for students and seekers of Islamic knowledge, my Shaykh has been working tirelessly to meet these demands. With a combination of Shaykh's unique style of teaching and his efforts of propagating the Deen of Allāh ﷻ and a desire to please Him, this book was made possible.

It is with deep regret that the youth of today spend their time wastefully in futile amusement that distracts them from their Creator, Allāh ﷻ. As a result of this, the youth begin distancing themselves further from the Deen. Our beloved Prophet ﷺ said, "Seeking knowledge is compulsory upon every Muslim." It is therefore very important that we educate ourselves, our loved ones, our children and our youth about Islām, Who our Creator is, and who Prophet Muhammad ﷺ is.

If we were to truly realise the importance Islām places on knowledge and its virtues, then we will definitely be keen to learn and teach others. We would start with ourselves, our families, then our neighbours and the community at large.

It is related by Imām Bukhāri and Imām Muslim 🕮 that once Sayyidunā Mu'āwiyah 🕮 gave a sermon in which he said, "I heard the Messenger of Allāh 🕮 saying, "If Allāh 🕮 intends goodness for a person, then He gives him the understanding of Deen."

It is quite shocking that if we were to ask a young child or an adult student to name just a few famous Companions of the Holy Prophet 🕮, they would struggle or would need to think about it, but when asked to name their favourite pop stars or football players, they would name them without hesitating!

With the above concerns in mind and to meet the desire to learn about our beautiful Deen, my Shaykh has put together this simple, educational book on the basic knowledge of Islām. The book is set out in such a way, where the reader or student will enjoy learning about Islām in the form of multiple questions.

It is the author's hope to introduce this book to our young children in Islamic schools and Madrasahs so that each child or adult student can cherish the treasures of knowledge they will learn. I am confident that this book will be a very beneficial tool if it is included in the educational syllabus. The book is also ideal for the whole family to learn new knowledge and facts about Islām in an enjoyable way!

I sincerely pray that this book becomes a fruitful educational tool in our homes, schools and Madrasahs for our children and adult students.

May Allāh ﷻ accept this precious book and reward my beloved teacher Shaykh Mufti Saiful Islām for his sacrifices and efforts in propagating the Deen of Allah ﷻ to the masses, and make it a means of salvation in this world and the Hereafter. Āmeen

I also pray to Allāh ﷻ that He preserves my Shaykh's health, his blessed knowledge and his intriguing wisdom, so that he can continue benefiting the Ummah.

محمد مجيب الرحمن

Muhammad Mujibur-Rahmān
Student of Jāmiah Khātamun Nabiyeen, Bradford, UK
10 Jumādath-Thāni 1432 / 5 May 2011

Beliefs

1. How many pillars does Islām stand on?
a) Four pillars
b) Five pillars
c) Six pillars

2. What does Islām mean?
a) Submission to Allāh ﷻ
b) Guidance
c) Path

3. What does Tawheed mean?
a) Ascribing partners to Allāh ﷻ
b) Obedience
c) Unity of Allāh ﷻ

4. What does Shirk mean?
a) Unity of Allāh ﷻ
b) Disobedience
c) Ascribing partners to Allāh ﷻ

5. What does Shahādah mean?
a) To bear witness
b) To purify
c) To obey

6. What does Taqdeer mean?
a) Happiness
b) Allāh's ﷻ knowledge of the creation before its creation
c) Allāh's ﷻ promise

7. When will the Day of Judgement take place?
a) After a long time
b) 2050
c) Only Allāh ﷻ knows

8. Who are the Kirāman Kātibeen?
a) The Angels who write the good and bad deeds
b) The Angels who question the dead
c) The Angel of death

9. What does Khātamun Nabiyyeen mean?
a) The best Prophet
b) The last Prophet
c) The first Prophet

10. Mu'jizah is a miracle shown by whom?
a) A prophet
b) A pious person
c) A non-Muslim

Angels

1. How many famous Angels are there?
a) Six
b) Four
c) Two

2. Which Angel is in charge of food and rain?
a) Sayyidunā Jibreel ﷺ
b) Sayyidunā Isrāfeel ﷺ
c) Sayyidunā Meekhāeel ﷺ

3. Which Angel will blow the trumpet?
a) Sayyidunā Isrāfeel ﷺ
b) Ridhwān
c) Munkar and Nakeer

4. Which Angel brought Allah's ﷻ Books?
a) Sayyidunā Izrā'eel ﷺ
b) Sayyidunā Jibreel ﷺ
c) Mālik

5. Do Angels commit sins?
a) Yes
b) No
c) Sometimes

6. Which Angels question a person when he dies?
a) Kirāman Kātibeen
b) Munkar and Nakeer
c) Hāroot and Māroot

7. Which Angel is in charge of Hell?
a) Sayyidunā Jibreel ﷺ
b) Ridhwān
c) Mālik

8. What are Angels made from?
a) Clay
b) Light
c) Fire

9. How many Angels are there?
a) 124,000
b) 1 million
c) Exact number not known

10. Which Angel is in charge of death?
a) Kirāman Kātibeen
b) Munkar and Nakeer
c) Sayyidunā Izrā'eel ﷺ

Books of Allāh ﷻ

1. Which Book did Sayyidunā Moosā ﷺ receive?
a) . Tawrah
b) Injeel
c) Zaboor

2. Which Book did Sayyidunā Dāwood ﷺ receive?
a) Tawrah
b) Zaboor
c) Saheefah

3. Where did the Holy Prophet ﷺ receive the 1st revelation?
a) Cave Thawr
b) Mount Uhud
c) Cave Hira

4. The first verses revealed are in which Sūrah?
a) Sūrah Al-Alaq
b) Sūrah Al-Fātihah
c) Sūrah Al-Baqarah

5. Which is the final Book revealed by Allāh ﷻ?
a) The Zaboor
b) The Injeel
c) The Holy Qur'ān

6. The Holy Qur'ān was revealed in a period of...
a) 40 years
b) 23 years
c) 10 years

7. In which month was the Holy Qur'ān revealed?
a) Ramadhān
b) Muharram
c) Safar

8. How many Sūrahs are there in the Holy Qur'ān?
a) 114
b) 141
c) 104

9. Which Sūrah is known as the heart of the Qur'ān?
a) Sūrah Al-Fātihah
b) Sūrah Yāseen
c) Sūrah Ar-Rahmān

10. Which is the longest Sūrah in the Holy Qur'ān?
a) Sūrah Al-Mulk
b) Sūrah An-Nās
c) Sūrah Al-Baqarah

Prophets of Allāh ﷺ

1. Which Prophet's nation was drowned by a flood?
a) Sayyidunā Sālih ﷺ
b) Sayyidunā Hūd ﷺ
c) Sayyidunā Nūh ﷺ

2. Which Prophet was the first human being?
a) Sayyidunā Nūh ﷺ
b) Sayyidunā Ibrāheem ﷺ
c) Sayyidunā Ādam ﷺ

3. Which Prophet was thrown into a well by his brothers?
a) Sayyidunā Yūsuf ﷺ
b) Sayyidunā Yaqūb ﷺ
c) Sayyidunā Lūt ﷺ

4. Which Prophet ruled the world?
a) Sayyidunā Zakariyyā ﷺ
b) Sayyidunā Eesā ﷺ
c) Sayyidunā Sulaimān ﷺ

5. Which Prophet's nation demanded a she-camel?
a) Sayyidunā Moosā ﷺ
b) Sayyidunā Dāwood ﷺ
c) Sayyidunā Sālih ﷺ

6. Which Prophet was ordered to sacrifice his own son?
a) Sayyidunā Ismā'eel ﷺ
b) Sayyidunā Ibrāheem ﷺ
c) Sayyidunā Shuaib ﷺ

7. Sayyidah Maryam ﷺ was the mother of which Prophet?
a) Sayyidunā Yahyā ﷺ
b) Sayyidunā Zakariyyā ﷺ
c) Sayyidunā Eesā ﷺ

8. Who is the most highly ranked Prophet?
a) Sayyidunā Ādam ﷺ
b) Prophet Muhammad ﷺ
c) Sayyidunā Ibrāheem ﷺ

9. Which Prophet will return to earth before Qiyāmah?
a) Sayyidunā Eesā ﷺ
b) Sayyidunā Moosā ﷺ
c) Sayyidunā Ishāq ﷺ

10. Which Prophet was swallowed by a fish?
a) Sayyidunā Yūsuf ﷺ
b) Sayyidunā Yahyā ﷺ
c) Sayyidunā Yūnus ﷺ

Cleanliness Part 1

b) Wājib
c) Fardh

1. Talking about worldly matters whilst doing Wudhu is...
a) Harām
b) Permissible
c) Makrooh

2. To clean the nose with the right hand is...
a) Permissible
b) Mustahab
c) Makrooh

3. To begin with the right hand in Wudhu is...
a) Mustahab
b) Permissible
c) Makrooh

4. Reciting Bismillāh in Wudhu is...
a) Fardh
b) Sunnat
c) Mustahab

5. Washing the face in Wudhu is...
a) Sunnat

6. Passing water into the nostrils in Ghusl (bath) is...
a) Fardh
b) Mustahab
c) Sunnat

7. Pouring water over the whole body thrice is...
a) Fardh
b) Sunnat
c) Mustahab

8. How many Fardh are there in Tayammum?
a) Three
b) Four
c) Five

9. Does bleeding break Wudhu?
a) Yes
b) No
c) Sometimes

10. Wudhu is permissible with..
a) Used water
b) Rain water
c) Water taken out from fruits

Cleanliness Part 2

1. Tayammum is permissible when...
a) It is hot weather
b) Salāh time is running out
c) Water is not available

2. What does Niyyat mean?
a) Intention
b) Sincerity
c) Du'ā

3. Tayammum is permissible with...
a) Wood
b) Metal
c) Stone

4. What does Najāsat Ghaleezah mean?
a) Light type of impurity
b) Heavy type of impurity
c) Close to Harām

5. What does Istinjā mean?
a) Performing Wudhu
b) Having a shower
c) Cleaning the private parts after the call of nature

6. Which hand should be used for Istinjā?
a) Any
b) Left
c) Right

7. What does Hadath mean?
a) Unclean
b) Sayings
c) In need of Wudhu or Ghusl

8. Niyyat in Wudhu is...
a) Fardh
b) Sunnat
c) Wājib

9. A traveller can do Masah on leather socks for...
a) 24 hours
b) 48 hours
c) 72 hours

10. Doing Masah of one quarter of the head is...
a) Wājib
b) Fardh
c) Mustahab

13

Salāh Part 1

1. To make Niyyat (intention) in Salāh is...
a) Fardh
b) Wājib
c) Sunnat

2. To recite Thanā (Subhānaka) in Salāh is...
a) Makrooh
b) Sunnat
c) Wājib

3. To recite Sūrah Al-Fātihah in Salāh is...
a) Wājib
b) Fardh
c) Nafl (optional)

4. Ruku in Salāh is...
a) Fardh
b) Sunnat
c) Mustahab

5. How many times should Tasbeeh of Ruku be done?
a) Odd number of times
b) Twice
c) Once

6. What does Qawmah mean?
a) To say Bismillāh
b) To stand up straight after Ruku
c) To concentrate

7. Āmeen in Salāh should be said...
a) Loudly
b) Softly
c) Silently

8. To recite Tashahhud (At-Tāhiyyātu) is...
a) Fardh
b) Sunnat
c) Wājib

9. To recite Durood Shareef in Salāh is...
a) Mustahab
b) Sunnat
c) Fardh

10. How many Rakāts are there in Witr Salāh?
a) Five
b) Four
c) Three

14

Salāh Part 2

1. How many Fardh Rakāts are there in Fajr Salāh?
a) Two
b) Four
c) Six

2. How many Rakāts are there in Tarāweeh?
a) Eight
b) Twelve
c) Twenty

3. What does Ruku mean?
a) To bow down
b) To prostrate
c) To stand

4. What does Jalsa mean?
a) Standing up after Ruku
b) Sitting between the two Sajdahs
c) Not rushing in Salāh

5. What does Qir'at mean?
a) Reciting the Holy Qur'ān
b) First sitting
c) Standing up after Ruku

6. Performing Salāh bare-headed is...
a) Permissible
b) Mustahab
c) Makrooh

7. To recite looking in the text of Holy Qur'ān in Sālah is...
a) Makrooh
b) Permissible
c) Not permissible

8. A Muqtadi is a person...
a) Who leads the Salāh
b) Who comes late to Salāh
c) Who follows the Imām

9. Salāh performed with Jamā'at is...
a) 10 times greater than performing Salāh alone
b) 50 times greater than performing Salāh alone
c) 27 times greater than performing Salāh alone

10. Who deserves to be an Imām?
a) The oldest person
b) The tallest person
c) The knowledgeable person

15

Salāh Part 3

1.   Jumu'ah Khutbah (sermon) must be performed...
a)   Before Salāh
b)   After Salāh
c)   In Salāh

2.   Jumu'ah Salāh is...
a)   Fardh
b)   Sunnat
c)   Wājib

3.   When is Jumu'ah Salah performed?
a)   At 12:00 pm
b)   After Zawāl
c)   After sunrise

4.   Salāh is compulsory...
a)   Five times a day
b)   Three times a day
c)   Two times a day

5.   How many Takbeers are there in the Janāzah Salāh?
a)   Three
b)   Five
c)   Four

6.   When is Sajdah Sahw performed?
a)   When you miss a Fardh act
b)   When you miss a Sunnat act
c)   When you miss a Wājib act

7.   Masbooq is a person who...
a)   Joins the Imām from the beginning of Salāh
b)   Joins the Imām after missing a Rakāt or more
c)   Performs the Salāh individually.

8.   When does a person become a Musāfir?
a)   After travelling 48 miles
b)   After travelling 16 miles
c)   After travelling 100 miles

9.   A Musāfir will make Qasr (shorten) of which Salāh?
a)   Fajr Salāh
b)   Maghrib Salāh
c)   Zuhr Salāh

10.   Male Kafn (shroud) consists of...
a)   Three pieces of cloth
b)   Two pieces of cloth
c)   Five pieces of cloth

16

Eid Salāh

1. Khutbah of Eid Salāh is...
a) Fardh
b) Sunnat
c) Wājib

2. Eid Salāh is performed...
a) Individually
b) In Jamā'at
c) At home

3. When is Eidul Fitr?
a) On the 1st of Shawwāl
b) On the 10th of Muharram
c) On the 27th of Rajab

4. How many extra Takbeers are there in the Eid Salāh?
a) Four
b) Eight
c) Six

5. How many Rakāts are there in the Eid Salāh?
a) Two
b) Four
c) Three

6. Eid Salāh is...
a) Wājib
b) Fardh
c) Sunnat

7. Is there Adhān and Iqāmat in the Eid Salāh?
a) Yes
b) No
c) Only Adhān

8. How many Eids are there each year?
a) Three
b) One
c) Two

9. When is Eidul Adhā?
a) On the 15th of Shabān
b) On the 1st of Muharram
c) On the 10th of Dhul Hijjah

10. When should Sadaqatul Fitr be given?
a) On Eidul Fitr
b) On Eidhul Adhā
c) On both Eids

Zakāt

1. To give Zakāt is...
a) Fardh
b) Wājib
c) Optional

2. What does Zakāt mean?
a) To submit
b) To make intention
c) To increase

3. At what rate is Zakāt given?
a) 25%
b) 5.5%
c) 2.5%

4. Upon whom is Zakāt Fardh?
a) Children
b) Adults
c) Muslim and non-Muslim

5. Niyyat for Zakāt is...
a) Fardh
b) Sunnat
c) Nafl

6. To whom can Zakāt be given?
a) To a hospital
b) To a poor person
c) To an old person

7. The amount of wealth which makes one liable for Zakāt is called...
a) Masraf
b) Nisāb
c) Lillāh

8. On what items is Zakāt Fardh?
a) On gold and silver
b) On clothes
c) On diamonds and pearls

9. Zakāt can be given to...
a) A wealthy person
b) Own children
c) Poor orphans

10. To whom can Sadaqatul Fitr be given?
a) To sons and daughters
b) To mother and father
c) To a poor student

Fasting Part 1

1. **In which month do we fast?**
a) Shawwāl
b) Muharram
c) Ramadhān

2. **Fasting in Ramadhān is..**
a) Fardh
b) Wājib
c) Sunnah

3. **What is the name of the special Salāh performed in Ramadhān?**
a) Tahajjud
b) Ishrāq
c) Tarāweeh

4. **The food eaten early in the morning before starting the fast is called...**
a) Snack
b) Iftār
c) Sahree

5. **We should open our fasts with...**
a) Somosas and Kebabs
b) Water and Dates
c) Rice and Curry

6. **Those who fast will enter through the door of...**
a) Firdous
b) Na'eem
c) Rayyān

7. **Using toothpaste whilst fasting is...**
a) Permissible
b) Makrooh
c) Mustahab

8. **The Kaffārah for breaking a Ramadhān fast intentionally is...**
a) 10 fasts
b) 30 fasts
c) 60 fasts

9. **Taking a bath will...**
a) Break the fast
b) Not break the fast
c) Reduce the reward

10. **Lailatul-Qadr (the Night of Power) occurs in the...**
A. 1st ten days of Ramadhān
B. 2nd ten days of Ramadhan
C. 3rd ten days of Ramadhān

19

Fasting Part 2

1. **To make Niyyat (intention) in fasting is...**
a) Fardh
b) Wājib
c) Sunnat

2. **To have Sahree before Subha Sādiq is...**
a) Mustahab
b) Sunnat
c) Wājib

3. **Tarāweeh Salāh is performed in...**
a) Ramadhān
b) Muharram
c) Special nights

4. **Tarāweeh Salāh is...**
a) Nafl
b) Sunnat
c) Wājib

5. **In Ramadhān, the reward of every act is multiplied by...**
a) 10 times
b) 70 times
c) 100 times

6. **The reward of every Nafl act in Ramadhān is equal to...**
a) A Fardh act
b) A Wājib act
c) A Sunnat act

7. **Ramadhān is the...**
a) First month of the Islamic calendar
b) Last month of the Islamic calendar
c) Ninth month of the Islamic calendar

8. **Itikāf in the last ten days of Ramadhān is...**
a) Fardh
b) Sunnat
c) Wājib

9. **Lailatul-Qadr (the Night of Power) is better than...**
a) 1000 months
b) 10 years
c) 1000 years

10. **Iftār should be done after...**
a) Tarāweeh
b) Maghrib Salāh
c) Sunset

20

Fasting Part 3

1. Which person is excused from fasting?
a) Student
b) Worker
c) Sick person

2. When does fasting begin?
a) From Subha Sādiq
b) From Sunrise
c) From Midnight

3. When does fasting finish?
a) At 5:00 pm
b) After school
c) Sunset

4. Upon whom is fasting compulsory?
a) Every male and female adult
b) Wealthy people
c) Those who perform Tarāweeh Salāh

5. Fasting teaches us to...
a) Save money
b) Think about the poor
c) Think about food

6. Fasting on the Day of Arafah is...
a) Makrooh
b) Fardh
c) Sunnah

7. If a Nafl fast is broken should it be kept?
a) Yes
b) No
c) It's optional

8. Which days did the Holy Prophet ﷺ normally fast?
a) Tuesdays and Wednesdays
b) Mondays and Thursdays
c) Weekends

9. Women should perform Itikāf in the...
a) Masjid
b) Homes
c) Should not perform Itikāf

10. Smoking whilst fasting...
a) Breaks the fast
b) Makes the fast Makrooh
c) Is permissible

21

Hajj Part 1

1. Hajj is the...
a) 1st pillar of Islām
b) 3rd pillar of Islām
c) 5th pillar of Islām

2. When is Hajj Fardh?
a) Every year
b) Once in a life time
c) When one is 40 years old

3. What is Qirān?
a) Umrah and Hajj performed with one Ihrām
b) To perform Umrah only
c) Hajj and Umrah performed with different Ihrāms

4. What is Tamattu?
a) To perform Umrah only
b) Stay in Makkah with Ihrām
c) To perform Hajj and Umrah with different Ihrāms

5. What is Ifrād?
a) To perform Hajj only
b) To perform Umrah only
c) To perform both Hajj and Umrah

6. How many times did
7. the Holy Prophet ﷺ perform Hajj?
a) Two times
b) One time
c) Three times

7. Tawāf Ziyārat is...
a) Fardh
b) Wājib
c) Sunnat

8. Tawāf Widāh is...
a) Sunnat
b) Fardh
c) Wājib

9. How many pebbles are thrown at each Jamarāt (Shaytān)?
a) Ten
b) Seven
c) Three

10. The Day of Arafah is on the...
a) 8th of Dhul Hijjah
b) 9thof Dhul Hijjah
c) 10th of Dhul Hijjah

22

Hajj Part 2

1. Upon whom is Hajj Fardh?
a) Wealthy people
b) Men only
c) Poor people

2. How many times is Tawāf done around the Ka'bah?
a) 10 times
b) 7 times
c) 14 times

3. What is the cloth worn by the pilgrim called?
a) Kafn
b) Jubbah
c) Ihrām

4. Wuqoof (staying) in Arafah is...
a) Fardh
b) Sunnat
c) Mustahab

5. Tawāf Qudoom is...
a) Fardh
b) Sunnat
c) Wājib

6. Where is the Holy Ka'bah?
a) In Madeenah
b) In Makkah
c) In Jerusalem

7. In which month is Hajj performed?
a) Ramadhān
b) Safar
c) Dhul Hijjah

8. The well of Zam Zam started from the time of...
a) Sayyidunā Ibrāheem عليه السلام
b) Prophet Muhammad ﷺ
c) Sayyidunā Ādam عليه السلام

9. On the 8th of Dhul Hijjah pilgrims go to...
a) Muzdalifah
b) Arafah
c) Minā

10. How many Jamarāts are there?
a) Two
b) Three
c) One

Hajj Part 3

1. Whilst in Ihrām it is permissible to...
a) Eat and drink
b) Cut nails
c) Use perfume

2. Sa'ee between Safā and Marwah is...
a) Fardh
b) Wājib
c) Sunnat

3. What does Ramal mean?
a) To walk quickly in the first 3 circuits of Tawāf
b) To kiss the black stone
c) To go around the Ka'bah

4. What does Istilām mean?
a) Exposing the right shoulder in Tawāf
b) Saying Labbaik
c) To kiss the black stone

5. To stay in Minā is...
a) Fardh
b) Wājib
c) Sunnat

6. Which animal can be sacrificed in Hajj?
a) Chicken
b) Sheep
c) Deer

7. The name of the water drank in Hajj is called...
a) Kawthar
b) Holy water
c) Zam Zam

8. In which Islamic year did the farewell Hajj take place?
a) 10th year of Prophethood
b) 9th year of Hijri
c) 10th year of Hijri

9. To kiss the black stone is...
a) Fardh
b) Sunnat
c) Wājib

10. How many times did the Holy Prophet ﷺ perform Umrah during his lifetime?
a) Four
b) Two
c) One

24

Islamic Terms Part 1

1.   What does Fardh mean?
a)   Compulsory
b)   Optional
c)   Recommended

2.   What does Harām mean?
a)   Disliked
b)   Forbidden
c)   Permissible

3.   What does Makrooh mean?
a)   Liked
b)   Disliked
c)   Necessary

4.   What does Mubāh mean?
a)   Optional
b)   Permissible
c)   Compulsory

5.   What does Mustahab mean?
a)   Recommended
b)   Compulsory
c)   Forbidden

6.   What does Masnoon mean?
a)   Preferable
b)   Practice of the Holy   Prophet 鑪
c)   Optional

7.   What does Muakkadah mean?
a)   Emphasised
b)   Not emphasised
c)   Praiseworthy

8.   What does Makrooh Tahreemi mean?
a)   Near to Harām
b)   Near to Halāl
c)   Disliked

9.   What does Najāsat   Khafeefah mean?
a)   Impure
b)   In need of Wudhu or bath
c)   Light type of impurity

10. What does Najāsat Haqeeqi mean?
a)   Impurity which can be seen
b)   Impurity which cannot be seen
c)   In need of Wudhu

25

Islamic Terms
Part 2

1. What does Tahmeed mean?
a) Allāhu Akbar
b) Rabbanā Lakal Hamd
c) Subhān-Allāh

2. What does Tasbeeh mean?
a) Lāilāha Illallāh
b) Samiallāhu Liman Hamida
c) Subhān-Allāh

3. What does Tahleel mean?
a) Lāilāha Illallāh
b) Alhamdulillāh
c) Māshā-Allāh

4. What does Takbeer mean?
a) Inshā Allāh
b) Allāhu Akbar
c) Innā Lillāh

5. What does Tasmee mean?
a) Samiallāhu Liman Hamida
b) Lāilāha Illallāh
c) Subhān-Allāh

6. What does Tajweed mean?
a) To run
b) To think of good things
c) To recite the Holy Qur'ān correctly.

7. What does Tawheed mean?
a) Unity of Allāh ﷻ
b) Belief in the Books
c) Prophethood

8. What does Tamjeed mean?
a) To praise Allāh ﷻ
b) To recite the Holy Qur'ān correctly
c) To believe in Allāh ﷻ

9. What does Tayyibah mean?
a) Pure
b) Clean
c) Fresh

10. What does Tasmiyah mean?
a) High
b) Stand
c) Bismillāhir Rahmānir - Raheem

Islamic Terms Part 3

1. Who is a Mufti?
a) A person who issues Fatwas
b) A person who leads the Salāh
c) A person who teaches in an Islamic school

2. Who is a Mufassir?
a) A person who leads the Salāh
b) A person who teaches the commentary of the Holy Qur'ān
c) A person who teaches Hadeeth

3. Who is a Qāri?
a) A person who recites the Holy Qur'ān with Tajweed
b) A person who knows the Ahādeeth
c) A person who leads the Salāh

4. Who is an Imām?
a) A person who recites the Holy Qur'ān with Tajweed
b) A person who issues Fatwas
c) A person who leads the Salāh

5. Who is a Muallim?
a) A person who leads the Salāh
b) A person who teaches in an Islamic school
c) A person who recites the Holy Qur'ān with Tajweed

6. Who is a Sahābi?
a) A person who saw the Holy Prophet
b) A person who recites the Holy Qur'ān with Tajweed
c) A person who leads the Salāh

7. Who is a Muhaddith?
a) A person who issues Fatwās
b) A person who leads the Salāh
c) A person who teaches the Ahādeeth

27

Islamic Terms
Part 3

Continued...

8.   Who is an Ālim?

a)   A person with Islamic knowledge

b)   A person who has memorised the Holy Qur'ān

c)   A person who teaches Ahādeeth

9.   Who is a Hāfiz?

a)   A person with Islamic knowledge

b)   A person who has memorised the Holy Qur'ān

c)   A person who knows the Ahādeeth

10.   Who is a Tābi'ee?

a)   A person who saw a Sahābi

b)   A person who has memorised the Holy Qur'ān

c)   A person who is a leader

Seerah Part 1

1. What did the people of Arabia worship before Islām?
a) Allāh
b) Idols
c) Three gods

2. In which month was the Holy Prophet born?
a) Rabee-ul-Awwal
b) Ramadhān
c) Muharram

3. Who was the Holy Prophet's father?
a) Abdullāh
b) Hamzah
c) Abū Tālib

4. Which tribe did the Holy Prophet belong to?
a) Banū Tameem
b) Banū Najjār
c) Quraish

5. Who was the mother of the Holy Prophet?
a) Haleemah
b) Āminah
c) Umme Ayman

6. Who was the Holy Prophet's first wife?
a) Sayyidah Ā'ishah
b) Sayyidah Khadeejah
c) Sayyidah Hafsah

7. At what age did the Holy Prophet marry Sayyidah Khadeejah?
a) Twenty five
b) Thirty
c) Thirty five

8. What was the title the people of Makkah gave to the Holy Prophet?
a) Al-Ameen
b) As-Sālih
c) Al-Basheer

Seerah Part 1

Continued...

9.   Which uncle looked after the Holy Prophet 繠 when he became an orphan?
a)   Abū Lahab
b)   Abū Tālib
c)   Abdul Muttalib

10.   At what age did the   Holy Prophet 繠 receive prophethood?
a)   Twenty five
b)   Forty
c)   Fifty

Seerah Part 2

1. In which year did Sayyidunā Umar ﷺ accept Islām?
a) 3rd year of prophethood
b) 6th year of prophethood
c) 10th year of prophethood

2. For how many years did the Quraish boycott the Holy Prophet ﷺ?
a) 3 years
b) 5 years
c) 7 years

3. When did Sayyidah Khadeejah ﷺ pass away?
a) In the 10th year of prophethood
b) In the 5th year of prophethood
c) In the 1st year of Hijri

4. What does Mi'rāj mean?
a) A puddle of water at a far distance
b) Salāh
c) Journey to the Heavens

5. At what age did the Holy Prophet ﷺ migrate to Madeenah?
a) 33 years old
b) 43 years old
c) 53 years old

6. When the enemies were chasing the Holy Prophet ﷺ at the time of Hijrah, where did he hide?
a) Cave of Thawr
b) Cave of Hirā
c) Holy Ka'bah

7. How many Muslims were there in the Battle of Badr?
a) 113
b) 313
c) 1,000

8. How many disbelievers were there in the Battle of Badr?
a) 113
b) 313
c) 1,000

Seerah Part 2

Continued...

9.   Which famous Companion became Shaheed in the Battle of Uhud?
a)   Sayyidunā Hamzah ﷺ
b)   Sayyidunā Sa'd ﷺ
c)   Sayyidunā Ali ﷺ

10.   When did the conquest (victory) of Makkah take place?
a)   5th year of Hijri
b)   8th year of Hijri
c)   10th year of Hijri

Seerah Part 3

1. When did the Battle of Uhud take place?
a) 5th year of Hijri
b) 3rd year of Hijri
c) 1st year of Hijri

2. The Sahābi who gave the idea of digging a trench in the Battle of Trench was...
a) Sayyidunā Hudhaifah ؓ
b) Sayyidunā Bilāl ؓ
c) Sayyidunā Salmān Fārsi ؓ

3. When did the treaty of Hudaibiyah take place?
a) 6th year of Hijri
b) 8th year of Hijri
c) 10th year of Hijri

4. When did the Battle of Tabūk take place?
a) 9th year of Hijri
b) 6th year of Hijri
c) 8th year of Hijri

5. The campaign of Tabūk took place because of the...
a) Persian Empire
b) Roman Empire
c) Disbelievers of Makkah

6. When did the Battle of Badr take place?
a) 1st year of Hijri
b) 2nd year of Hijri
c) 3rd year of Hijri

7. In which month did the Holy Prophet ﷺ pass away?
a) Rabbee-ul-Awwal
b) Ramadhān
c) Shawwāl

8. Who was the first Caliph after the death of the Holy Prophet ﷺ?
a) Sayyidunā Umar ؓ
b) Sayyidunā Uthmān ؓ
c) Sayyidunā Abū Bakr ؓ

Seerah Part 3

Continued...

**9. Where is the Holy Prophet
ﷺ buried?**
a) Madeenah
b) Makkah
c) Baitul Maqdis

**10. At what age was the demise
of the Holy Prophet ﷺ?**
a) At the age of 40
b) At the age of 53
c) At the age of 63

The Wives of the Holy Prophet ﷺ

1. Name the daughter of Sayyidunā Umar 🏵 who married the Holy Prophet ﷺ?
a) Sayyidah Zainab 🏵
b) Sayyidah Khadeejah 🏵
c) Sayyidah Hafsah 🏵

2. Name the wife who was also the cousin sister of the Holy Prophet ﷺ?
a) Sayyidah Zainab Bint Jahash 🏵
b) Sayyidah Ā'ishah 🏵
c) Sayyidah Maymūnah 🏵

3. Name the wife who was the sister of Sayyidunā Muāwiyah 🏵?
a) Sayyidah Umme Salamah 🏵
b) Sayyidah Umme Habeebah 🏵
c) Sayyidah Sawdah 🏵

4. Who was the first wife to pass away?
a) Sayyidah Khadeejah 🏵
b) Sayyidah Sawdah 🏵
c) Sayyidah Ā'ishah 🏵

5. At what age did Sayyidah Khadeejah 🏵 marry the Holy Prophet ﷺ?
a) 30 years old
b) 40 years old
c) 50 years old

6. At what age did Sayyidah Khadeejah 🏵 pass away?
a) At the age of 55
b) At the age of 65
c) At the age of 75

7. Who was the most knowledgeable wife of the Holy Prophet ﷺ?
a) Sayyidah Ā'ishah 🏵
b) Sayyidah Umme Salamah 🏵
c) Sayyidah Hafsah 🏵

35

The Wives of the Holy Prophet ﷺ

Continued...

8. **Before the marriage to the Holy Prophet ﷺ, Sayyidah Umme Salamah ؓ was married to...**
a) Sayyidunā Abū Salamah ؓ
b) Sayyidunā Abū Bakr ؓ
c) Sayyidunā Abū Hurairah ؓ

9. **Sayyidah Juwairiyah ؓ was the daughter of...**
a) A chief
b) A businessman
c) A poet

10. **Sayyidah Ā'ishah ؓ was the daughter of which famous Sahābi?**
a) Sayyidunā Uthmān ؓ
b) Sayyidunā Talhah ؓ
c) Sayyidunā Abū Bakr ؓ

The Companions
Part 1

1. Sayyidunā Abū Bakr ؓ was the…
a) 1st Caliph of Islām
b) 2nd Caliph of Islām
c) 4th Caliph of Islam

2. Sayyidunā Umar ؓ was the…
a) 4th Caliph of Islām
b) 3rd Caliph of Islām
c) 2nd Caliph of Islām

3. Which Sahābi was fortunate to marry two daughters of the Holy Prophet ﷺ one after another?
a) Sayyidunā Talhah ؓ
b) Sayyidunā Uthmān ؓ
c) Sayyidunā Sa'd ؓ

4. Sayyidah Fātimah ؓ was married to…
a) Sayyidunā Ali ؓ
b) Sayyidunā Jābir ؓ
c) Sayyidunā Abū Ubaidah ؓ

5. The only Sahābi mentioned in the Holy Qur'ān by name is…
a) Sayyidunā Zayd ؓ
b) Sayyidunā Abū Bakr ؓ
c) Sayyidunā Abū Hurairah ؓ

6. The Sahābi who narrated the most Ahādeeth was…
a) Sayyidah Ā'ishah ؓ
b) Sayyidunā Abdullāh Ibn Abbās ؓ
c) Sayyidunā Abū Hurairah ؓ

7. In which battle was Sayyidunā Musab Ibn Umair ؓ martyred?
a) Battle of Badr
b) Battle of Uhud
c) Battle of the Trench

8. Which Sahābi was known as the Sword of Allāh?
a) Sayyidunā Salamah ؓ
b) Sayyidunā Ali ؓ
c) Sayyidunā Khālid Ibn Waleed ؓ

The Companions
Part 1

Continued...

**9.   Sayyidunā Abbās ﷺ was the
Holy Prophet's ﷺ...**
a)   Uncle
b)   Brother
c)   Cousin

**10.   What was Sayyidunā Anas
ﷺ well known for?**
a)   His service to the Holy
Prophet ﷺ
b)   His bravery
c)   His poetry

The Companions Part 2

1. Who was the first adult male to accept Islām?

a) Sayyidunā Abū Bakr ⊛
b) Sayyidunā Umar ⊛
c) Sayyidunā Uthmān ⊛

2. Who was the first child to accept Islām?

a) Sayyidunā Zaid Ibn Thābit ⊛
b) Sayyidunā Ali ⊛
c) Sayyidunā Sa'd ⊛

3. Who was the first to accept Islām from the slaves?

a) Sayyidunā Bilāl ⊛
b) Sayyidunā Zaid Ibn Hārithah ⊛
c) Sayyidunā Salmān Fārsi ⊛

4. Who was the first adult female to accept Islām?

a) Sayyidah Ā'ishah ⊛
b) Sayyidah Hafsah ⊛
c) Sayyidah Khadeejah ⊛

5. Who was the first female Companion to be martyred?

a) Sayyidah Umme Salamah ⊛
b) Sayyidah Summayyah ⊛
c) Sayyidah Zainab ⊛

6. Who was the first Companion to call out the Adhān from the Ka'bah?

a) Sayyidunā Ali ⊛
b) Sayyidunā Zubair ⊛
c) Sayyidunā Bilāl ⊛

7. Who was the first woman Companion to memorise the Holy Qur'ān?

a) Sayyidah Ā'ishah ⊛
b) Sayyidah Zainab ⊛
c) Sayyidah Hafsah ⊛

8. Which Companion was known as the most trustworthy person of this Ummah?

a) Sayyidunā Ali ⊛
b) Sayyidunā Khālid Ibn Waleed ⊛
c) Sayyidunā Abū Ubaidah ⊛

The Companions
Part 2

Continued...

**9.   Which Companion was
well known in following
the Sunnah?**

a)   Sayyidunā Abū Hurairah ﷺ
b)   Sayyidunā Abdullāh
      Ibn Abbās ﷺ
c)   Sayyidunā Abdullāh
      Ibn Umar ﷺ

**10.   Which Companion was
known to be the most strict
in matters of Religion?**

a)   Sayyidunā Uthmān ﷺ
b)   Sayyidunā Zubair ﷺ
c)   Sayyidunā Umar ﷺ

The Companions Part 3

1. Who was the Holy Prophet's ﷺ adopted son?
a) Sayyidunā Anas ؓ
b) Sayyidunā Jābir ؓ
c) Sayyidunā Zaid ؓ

2. On the occasion of Mi'rāj, the Holy Prophet ﷺ heard the footsteps of which Companion?
a) Sayyidunā Bilāl ؓ
b) Sayyidunā Ali ؓ
c) Sayyidunā Umar ؓ

3. Which Companion's opinion was revealed in the Holy Qur'ān more than twenty times?
a) Sayyidunā Abū Bakr ؓ
b) Sayyidunā Umar ؓ
c) Sayyidunā Uthmān ؓ

4. Which Sahābi was the poet of the Holy Prophet ﷺ?
a) Sayyidunā Abū Hurairah ؓ
b) Sayyidunā Hassān Ibn Thābit ؓ
c) Sayyidunā Abdullāh Ibn Masood ؓ

5. Which daughter of the Holy Prophet ﷺ will be the leader of the ladies in Jannah?
a) Sayyidah Fātimah ؓ
b) Sayyidah Zainab ؓ
c) Sayyidah Ruqayyah

6. Who was one of the most wealthiest Sahābah?
a) Sayyidunā Talhā ؓ
b) Sayyidunā Sa'd ؓ
c) Sayyidunā Abdur-Rahmān Ibn Auf ؓ

7. Which Sahābi used to recite the entire Qur'ān in one Rak'at?
a) Sayyidunā Ali ؓ
b) Sayyidunā Uthmān ؓ
c) Sayyidunā Abū Dardā ؓ

The Companions
Part 3

Continued...

8. **Which Sahābi used to recite Istighfār 12,000 times daily?**
a) Sayyidunā Abū Hurairah ﷺ
b) Sayyidunā Abū Dardā ﷺ
c) Sayyidunā Zubair ﷺ

9. **Which Sahābi's face resembled that of the Holy Prophet ﷺ?**
a) Sayyidunā Ammār ﷺ
b) Sayyidunā Hasan ﷺ
c) Sayyidunā Abdullāh Ibn Masood ﷺ

10. **Who was a Jewish scholar before accepting Islām?**
a) Sayyidunā Abū Sufyān ﷺ
b) Sayyidunā Amr Ibn Ās ﷺ
c) Sayyidunā Abdullāh Ibn Salām ﷺ

The Companions Part 4

1. Who is the highest ranked Sahābi?
a) Sayyidunā Umar ؓ
b) Sayyidunā Abū Bakr ؓ
c) Sayyidunā Zubair ؓ

2. Who was the first Muad-dhin in Islām?
a) Sayyidunā Bilāl ؓ
b) Sayyidunā Ali ؓ
c) Sayyidunā Talhā ؓ

3. What does Asharah Mu-bassharah mean?
a) Ten Companions of the Holy Prophet ﷺ given glad tidings of Paradise
b) Ten Prophets of Allāh ﷻ
c) The four great Imāms

4. Who was the Sahābi who could run faster than a horse?
a) Sayyidunā Hamzah ؓ
b) Sayyidunā Salamah Ibn Ak'wa ؓ
c) Sayyidunā Ali ؓ

5. Who is the fourth Caliph of Islām?
a) Sayyidunā Uthmān ؓ
b) Sayyidunā Ali ؓ
c) Sayyidunā Zubair ؓ

6. Which Sahābi was well known for being just?
a) Sayyidunā Ali ؓ
b) Sayyidunā Sa'd ؓ
c) Sayyidunā Bilāl ؓ

7. Who is the third Caliph of Islām?
a) Sayyidunā Talha ؓ
b) Sayyidunā Umar ؓ
c) Sayyidunā Uthmān ؓ

8. Who shot the first arrow in Islām?
a) Sayyidunā Abū Bakr ؓ
b) Sayyidunā Sa'd ؓ
c) Sayyidunā Umar ؓ

9. Which Sahābi conquered Masjid Al-Aqsa?
a) Sayyidunā Khālid Ibn Waleed ؓ
b) Sayyidunā Ali ؓ
c) Sayyidunā Umar ؓ

The Companions
Part 4

Continued...

10.　What do we say when we mention a Sahābi?

a)　Radhiyallāhu anhu
b)　Rahmatullāhi alayh
c)　Alayhis Salām

Islamic Months

1. The first Islamic month is...
a) Ramadhān
b) Muharram
c) Shawwāl

2. Which is the most virtuous month of the year?
a) Dhul-Hijjah
b) Safar
c) Ramadhān

3. Which is the last month of the year?
a) Rabee-ul Awwāl
b) Rajab
c) Dhul-Hijjah

4. In which month is Hajj performed?
a) Shawwāl
b) Sha'bān
c) Dhul-Hijjah

5. In which month was the Holy Qur'ān revealed?
a) Ramadhān
b) Dhul-Hijjah
c) Rabeeul-Ākhir

6. In which month does Laylatul-Barā'at take place?
a) Ramadhān
b) Sha'bān
c) Jumādal-Oola

7. In which month does Lailatul-Qadr take place?
a) Sha'bān
b) Safar
c) Ramadhān

8. The Holy Prophet ﷺ kept the most fasts in which month after Ramadhān?
a) Dhul-Qa'dha
b) Dhul-Hijjah
c) Sha'bān

9. In which month was the Holy Prophet ﷺ born?
a) Ramadhān
b) Rabeeul-Awwal
c) Rajab

10. In which month does Qurbāni (sacrifice) take place?
a) Shawwāl
b) Muharram
c) Dhul-Hijjah

General Knowledge

1. **A Muslim's place of worship is called a...**
a) Madrasah
b) Markaz
c) Masjid

2. **What does Istighfār mean?**
a) Seeking the truth
b) Success
c) Seeking forgiveness

3. **Which is the most authentic book of Ahādeeth?**
a) Bukhāri
b) Muslim
c) Abū Dāwood

4. **Which day is the most virtuous day of the week?**
a) Monday
b) Friday
c) Sunday

5. **From what age did the Holy Prophet ﷺ order children to pray Salāh?**
a) Seven
b) Ten
c) Fifteen

6. **How many daughters did the Holy Prophet ﷺ have?**
a) Two daughters
b) Four daughters
c) Six daughters

7. **Which great Muslim conqueror liberated Masjid Al-Aqsa?**
a) Salāh-ud-Deen Ayyūbi
b) Muhammad Ibn Qāsim
c) Sultān Tipu

8. **Imām Abū Yūsuf and Imām Muhammad were two famous students of...**
a) Imām Shāfi'ee
b) Imām Mālik
c) Imām Abū Haneefah

General Knowledge

Continued...

9.   Ilmul Ghaib is exclusive to...
a)   Allāh 🕌
b)   Allāh 🕌 and the Holy Prophet 🕌
c)   Allāh 🕌 and the Angels

10.   The recitation of which Sūrah is safety from Dajjāl?
a)   Sūrah Al-Baqarah
b)   Sūrah Al-Kahf
c)   Sūrah Yāseen

47

Beliefs	Books of Allāh	Cleanliness Part 1	Salāh Part 1
Page 8	Page 10	Page 12	Page 14
1 = b	1 = a	1 = c	1 = a
2 = a	2 = b	2 = c	2 = b
3 = c	3 = c	3 = a	3 = a
4 = c	4 = a	4 = b	4 = a
5 = a	5 = c	5 = c	5 = a
6 = b	6 = b	6 = a	6 = b
7 = c	7 = a	7 = b	7 = b
8 = a	8 = a	8 = a	8 = c
9 = b	9 = b	9 = a	9 = b
10 = a	10 = c	10 = b	10 = c

Angels	Prophets of Allāh	Cleanliness Part 2	Salāh Part 2
Page 9	Page 11	Page 13	Page 15
1 = b	1 = c	1 = c	1 = a
2 = c	2 = c	2 = a	2 = c
3 = a	3 = a	3 = c	3 = a
4 = b	4 = c	4 = b	4 = b
5 = b	5 = c	5 = c	5 = a
6 = b	6 = b	6 = b	6 = c
7 = c	7 = c	7 = c	7 = c
8 = b	8 = b	8 = b	8 = c
9 = c	9 = a	9 = c	9 = c
10 = c	10 = c	10 = b	10 = c

Salāh Part 3	**Zakāt**	**Fasting Part 2**	**Hajj Part 1**
Page 16	Page 18	Page 20	Page 22
1 = a	1 = a	1 = a	1 = c
2 = a	2 = c	2 = b	2 = b
3 = b	3 = c	3 = a	3 = a
4 = a	4 = b	4 = b	4 = c
5 = c	5 = a	5 = b	5 = a
6 = c	6 = b	6 = a	6 = b
7 = b	7 = b	7 = c	7 = a
8 = a	8 = a	8 = b	8 = c
9 = c	9 = c	9 = a	9 = b
10 = a	10 = c	10 = c	10 = b

Eid Salāh	**Fasting Part 1**	**Fasting Part 3**	**Hajj Part 2**
Page 17	Page 19	Page 21	Page 23
1 = b	1 = c	1 = c	1 = a
2 = b	2 = a	2 = a	2 = b
3 = a	3 = c	3 = c	3 = c
4 = c	4 = c	4 = a	4 = a
5 = a	5 = b	5 = b	5 = b
6 = a	6 = c	6 = c	6 = b
7 = b	7 = b	7 = a	7 = c
8 = c	8 = c	8 = b	8 = a
9 = c	9 = b	9 = b	9 = c
10 = a	10 = c	10 = a	10 = b

Hajj Part 3

Page 24

1 = a
2 = b
3 = a
4 = c
5 = c
6 = b
7 = c
8 = c
9 = b
10 = a

Islamic Terms Part 2

Page 26

1 = b
2 = c
3 = a
4 = b
5 = a
6 = c
7 = a
8 = a
9 = a
10 = c

Seerah Part 1

Page 29

1 = b
2 = a
3 = a
4 = c
5 = b
6 = b
7 = a
8 = a
9 = b
10 = b

Seerah Part 3

Page 33

1 = b
2 = c
3 = a
4 = a
5 = b
6 = b
7 = a
8 = c
9 = a
10 = c

Islamic Terms Part 1

Page 25

1 = a
2 = b
3 = b
4 = b
5 = a
6 = b
7 = a
8 = a
9 = c
10 = a

Islamic Terms Part 3

Page 27

1 = a
2 = b
3 = a
4 = c
5 = b
6 = a
7 = c
8 = a
9 = b
10 = a

Seerah Part 2

Page 31

1 = b
2 = a
3 = a
4 = c
5 = c
6 = a
7 = b
8 = c
9 = a
10 = b

Wives of the Holy Prophet

Page 35

1 = c
2 = a
3 = b
4 = a
5 = b
6 = b
7 = a
8 = a
9 = a
10 = c

The Companions Part 1	The Companions Part 3	Islamic Months
Page 37	Page 41	Page 45
1 = a	1 = c	1 = b
2 = c	2 = a	2 = c
3 = b	3 = b	3 = c
4 = a	4 = b	4 = c
5 = a	5 = a	5 = a
6 = c	6 = c	6 = b
7 = b	7 = b	7 = c
8 = c	8 = a	8 = c
9 = a	9 = b	9 = b
10 = a	10 = c	10 = c

The Companions Part 2	The Companions Part 4	General Knowledge
Page 39	Page 43	Page 46
1 = a	1 = b	1 = c
2 = b	2 = a	2 = c
3 = b	3 = a	3 = a
4 = c	4 = b	4 = b
5 = b	5 = b	5 = a
6 = c	6 = a	6 = b
7 = a	7 = c	7 = a
8 = c	8 = b	8 = c
9 = c	9 = c	9 = a
10 = c	10 = a	10 = b

Scores:
How well did you do?

0 - 150 = Poor
150 - 200 = Average
200 - 250 = Good

250 - 275 = Very Good
275 - 300 = Excellent

Other titles from JKN Publications

Your Questions Answered

An outstanding book written by Shaykh Mufti Saiful Islām. A very comprehensive yet simple Fatāwa book and a source of guidance that reaches out to a wider audience i.e. the English speaking Muslims. The reader will benefit from the various answers to questions based on the Laws of Islām relating to the beliefs of Islām, knowledge, Sunnah, pillars of Islām, marriage, divorce and contemporary issues.

UK RRP: £7.50

Hadeeth for Beginners

A concise Hadeeth book with various Ahādeeth that relate to basic Ibādāh and moral etiquettes in Islām accessible to a wider readership. Each Hadeeth has been presented with the Arabic text, its translation and commentary to enlighten the reader, its meaning and application in day-to-day life.

UK RRP: £3.00

Du'ā for Beginners

This book contains basic Du'ās which every Muslim should recite on a daily basis. Highly recommended to young children and adults studying at Islamic schools and Madrasahs so that one may cherish the beautiful treasure of supplications of our beloved Prophet ﷺ in one's daily life, which will ultimately bring peace and happiness in both worlds, Inshā-Allāh.

UK RRP: £2.00

How well do you know Islām?

An exciting educational book which contains 300 multiple questions and answers to help you increase your knowledge on Islām! Ideal for the whole family, especially children and adult students to learn new knowledge in an enjoyable way and cherish the treasures of knowledge that you will acquire from this book. A very beneficial tool for educational syllabus.

UK RRP: £3.00

Treasures of the Holy Qur'ān

This book entitled "Treasures of the Holy Qur'ān" has been compiled to create a stronger bond between the Holy Qur'ān and the readers. It mentions the different virtues of Sūrahs and verses from the Holy Qur'ān with the hope that the readers will increase their zeal and enthusiasm to recite and inculcate the teachings of the Holy Qur'ān into their daily lives.

UK RRP: £3.00

Other titles from JKN PUBLICATIONS

Marriage - A Complete Solution

Islām regards marriage as a great act of worship. This book has been designed to provide the fundamental teachings and guidelines of all what relates to the marital life in a simplified English language. It encapsulates in a nutshell all the marriage laws mentioned in many of the main reference books in order to facilitate their understanding and implementation.

UK RRP: £5.00

Pearls of Luqmān

This book is a comprehensive commentary of Sūrah Luqmān, written beautifully by Shaykh Mufti Saiful Islām. It offers the reader with an enquiring mind, abundance of advice, guidance, counselling and wisdom.

The reader will be enlightened by many wonderful topics and anecdotes mentioned in this book, which will create a greater understanding of the Holy Qur'ān and its wisdom. The book highlights some of the wise sayings and words of advice Luqmān ﷺ gave to his son.

UK RRP: £3.00

Arabic Grammar for Beginners

This book is a study of Arabic Grammar based on the subject of Nahw (Syntax) in a simplified English format. If a student studies this book thoroughly, he/she will develop a very good foundation in this field, Inshā-Allāh. Many books have been written on this subject in various languages such as Arabic, Persian and Urdu. However, in this day and age there is a growing demand for this subject to be available in English .

UK RRP: £3.00

A Gift to My Youngsters

This treasure filled book, is a collection of Islamic stories, morals and anecdotes from the life of our beloved Prophet ﷺ, his Companions ﷺ and the pious predecessors. The stories and anecdotes are based on moral and ethical values, which the reader will enjoy sharing with their peers, friends, families and loved ones.

"A Gift to My Youngsters" – is a wonderful gift presented to the readers personally, by the author himself, especially with the youngsters in mind. He has carefully selected stories and anecdotes containing beautiful morals, lessons and valuable knowledge and wisdom.

UK RRP: £5.00

Travel Companion

The beauty of this book is that it enables a person on any journey, small or distant or simply at home, to utilise their spare time to read and benefit from an exciting and vast collection of important and interesting Islamic topics and lessons. Written in simple and easy to read text, this book will immensely benefit both the newly interested person in Islām and the inquiring mind of a student expanding upon their existing knowledge. Inspiring reminders from the Holy Qur'ān and the blessed words of our beloved Prophet ﷺ beautifies each topic and will illuminate the heart of the reader.   **UK RRP: £5.00**

Pearls of Wisdom

Junaid Baghdādi ﷺ once said, "Allāh ﷻ strengthens through these Islamic stories the hearts of His friends, as proven from the Qur'anic verse,
"And all that We narrate unto you of the stories of the Messengers, so as to strengthen through it your heart." (11:120)
Mālik Ibn Dinār ﷺ stated that such stories are gifts from Paradise. He also emphasised to narrate these stories as much as possible as they are gems and it is possible that an individual might find a truly rare and invaluable gem among them.   **UK RRP: £6.00**

Inspirations

This book contains a compilation of selected speeches delivered by Shaykh Mufti Saiful Islām on a variety of topics such as the Holy Qur'ān, Nikāh and eating Halāl. Having previously been compiled in separate booklets, it was decided that the transcripts be gathered together in one book for the benefit of the reader. In addition to this, we have included in this book, further speeches which have not yet been printed.

UK RRP: £6.00

Gift to my Sisters

A thought provoking compilation of very interesting articles including real life stories of pious predecessors, imaginative illustrations and much more. All designed to influence and motivate mothers, sisters, wives and daughters towards an ideal Islamic lifestyle. A lifestyle referred to by our Creator, Allāh ﷻ in the Holy Qur'ān as the means to salvation and ultimate success.

UK RRP: £6.00

Gift to my Brothers

A thought provoking compilation of very interesting articles including real life stories of pious predecessors, imaginative illustrations, medical advices on intoxicants and rehabilitation and much more. All designed to influence and motivate fathers, brothers, husbands and sons towards an ideal Islamic lifestyle. A lifestyle referred to by our Creator, Allāh ﷻ in the Holy Qur'ān as the means to salvation and ultimate success.

UK RRP: £5.00

Heroes of Islām

"In the narratives there is certainly a lesson for people of intelligence (understanding)." (12:111)

A fine blend of Islamic personalities who have been recognised for leaving a lasting mark in the hearts and minds of people.

A distinguishing feature of this book is that the author has selected not only some of the most world and historically famous renowned scholars but also these lesser known and a few who have simply left behind a valuable piece of advice to their nearest and dearest.   **UK RRP: £5.00**

Ask a Mufti (3 volumes)

Muslims in every generation have confronted different kinds of challenges. In-spite of that, Islām produced such luminary Ulamā who confronted and re-sponded to the challenges of their time to guide the Ummah to the straight path. "Ask A Mufti" is a comprehensive three volume fatwa book, based on the Hanafi School, covering a wide range of topics related to every aspect of human life such as belief, ritual worship, life after death and contemporary legal topics related to purity, commercial transaction, marriage, divorce, food, cosmetic, laws pertaining to women, Islamic medical ethics and much more.

UK RRP: £30.00

Should I Follow a Madhab?

Taqleed or following one of the four legal schools is not a new phenomenon. Historically, scholars of great calibre and luminaries, each one being a specialist in his own right, were known to have adhered to one of the four legal schools. It is only in the previous century that a minority group emerged advocating a se-vere ban on following one of the four major schools.

This book endeavours to address the topic of Taqleed and elucidates its im-portance and necessity in this day and age. It will also, by the Divine Will of Allāh ﷻ dispel some of the confusion surrounding this topic.   **UK RRP: £5.00**

Advice for the Students of Knowledge

Allāh ﷻ describes divine knowledge in the Holy Qur'ān as a 'Light'. Amongst the qualities of light are purity and guidance. The Holy Prophet ﷺ has clearly ex-plained this concept in many blessed Ahādeeth and has also taught us many supplications in which we ask for beneficial knowledge.

This book is a golden tool for every sincere student of knowledge wishing to mould his/her character and engrain those correct qualities in order to be wor-thy of receiving the great gift of Ilm from Allāh ﷻ.   **UK RRP: £3.00**

Stories for Children

"Stories for Children" - is a wonderful gift presented to the readers personally by the author himself, especially with the young children in mind. The stories are based on moral and ethical values, which the reader will enjoy sharing with their peers, friends, families and loved ones. The aim is to present to the children stories and incidents which contain moral lessons, in order to reform and correct their lives, according to the Holy Qur'ān and Sunnah.

UK RRP: £5.00

Pearls from My Shaykh

This book contains a collection of pearls and inspirational accounts of the Holy Prophet 鷺, his noble Companions, pious predecessors and some personal accounts and sayings of our well-known contemporary scholar and spiritual guide, Shaykh Mufti Saiful Islām Sāhib. Each anecdote and narrative of the pious predecessors have been written in the way that was narrated by Mufti Saiful Islām Sāhib in his discourses, drawing the specific lessons he intended from telling the story. The accounts from the life of the Shaykh has been compiled by a particular student based on their own experience and personal observation. **UK RRP: £5.00**

Paradise & Hell

This book is a collection of detailed explanation of Paradise and Hell including the state and conditions of its inhabitants. All the details have been taken from various reliable sources. The purpose of its compilation is for the reader to contemplate and appreciate the innumerable favours, rewards, comfort and unlimited luxuries of Paradise and at the same time take heed from the punishment of Hell. Shaykh Mufti Saiful Islām Sāhib has presented this book in a unique format by including the Tafseer and virtues of Sūrah Ar-Rahmān. **UK RRP: £5.00**

Prayers for Forgiveness

Prayers for Forgiveness' is a short compilation of Du'ās in Arabic with English translation and transliteration. This book can be studied after 'Du'ā for Beginners' or as a separate book. It includes twenty more Du'ās which have not been mentioned in the previous Du'ā book. It also includes a section of Du'ās from the Holy Qur'ān and a section from the Ahādeeth. The book concludes with a section mentioning the Ninety-Nine Names of Allāh 鷺 with its translation and transliteration. **UK RRP: £3.00**

Scattered Pearls

This book is a collection of scattered pearls taken from books, magazines, emails and WhatsApp messages. These pearls will hopefully increase our knowledge, wisdom and make us realise the purpose of life. In this book, Mufti Sāhib has included messages sent to him from scholars, friends and colleagues which will be beneficial and interesting for our readers Inshā-Allāh. **UK RRP: £4.00**

Poems of Wisdom

This book is a collection of poems from those who contributed to the Al-Mumin Magazine in the poems section. The Hadeeth mentions "Indeed some form of poems are full of wisdom." The themes of each poem vary between wittiness, thought provocation, moral lessons, emotional to name but a few. The readers will benefit from this immensely and make them ponder over the outlook of life in general.

UK RRP: £4.00

This book is a detailed and informative commentary of the first three Sūrahs of the last Juz namely; Sūrah Naba, Sūrah Nāzi'āt and Sūrah Abasa. These Sūrahs vividly depict the horrific events and scenes of the Great Day in order to warn mankind the end of this world. These Sūrahs are an essential reminder for us all to instil the fear and concern of the Day of Judgement and to detach ourselves from the worldly pleasures. Reading this book allows us to attain the true realization of this world and provides essential advices of how to gain eternal salvation in the Hereafter.

RRP: £5:00

It is necessary that Muslims always strive to better themselves at all times and to free themselves from the destructive maladies. This book focusses on three main spiritual maladies; pride, anger and evil gazes. It explains its root causes and offers some spiritual cures. Many examples from the lives of the pious predecessors are used for inspiration and encouragement for controlling the above three maladies. It is hoped that the purification process of the heart becomes easy once the underlying roots of the above maladies are clearly understood.   **UK RRP: £5:00**

This book is a step by step guide on Hajj and Umrah for absolute beginners. Many other additional important rulings (Masāil) have been included that will Insha-Allāh prove very useful for our readers. The book also includes some etiquettes of visiting (Ziyārat) of the Holy Prophet's 鷺 blessed Masjid and his Holy Grave.

UK   RRP   £3:00

This book contains essential guidelines for a spiritual Mureed to gain some familiarity of the science of Tasawwuf. It explains the meaning and aims of Tasawwuf, some understanding around the concept of the soul, and general guidelines for a spiritual Mureed. This is highly recommended book and it is hoped that it gains wider readership among those Mureeds who are basically new to the science of Tasawwuf.

UK RRP £3:00

This book is a compilation of sayings and earnest pieces of advice that have been gathered directly from my respected teacher Shaykh Mufti Saiful Islām Sāhib. The book consists of many valuable enlightenments including how to deal with challenges of life, promoting unity, practicing good manners, being optimistic and many other valuable advices. Our respected Shaykh has gathered this Naseehah from meditating, contemplating, analysing and searching for the gems within Qur'anic verses, Ahādeeth and teachings of our Pious Predecessors. **UK RRP £1:00**